TWO TREES
OF DESTINY

TWO TREES OF DESTINY

Louis J. Keroack

Library of Congress Control Number:		2012913295
ISBN:	Hardcover	978-1-4771-4951-5
	Softcover	978-1-4771-4950-8
	Ebook	978-1-4771-4952-2

To order additional copies of this book, contact:
Xlibris Corporation
1-888-795-4274
www.Xlibris.com
Orders@Xlibris.com

To Dr. Arnold Murray

Pastor of Shepherd's Chapel

Gravette, Arkansas

The dedication off this book will come as a complete surprise to Dr. Arnold Murray. Dr. Murray has no idea this book is being written by one of his loyal students at the age of ninety-two years young, a veteran of the Second World War, US Army Air Force.

I was very fortunate to meet up with a pastor who taught the Bible book by book, chapter by chapter, verse by verse, line by line, and precept upon precept.

I wish that all readers would get acquainted with this Web site: www. shepherdschapel.com

CONTENTS

BOOK TEMPLATE FOR LOUIS J. KEROACK

Coming out of the gate. I have always thought the wisdom of men is foolishness compared to the wisdom of God.

Every word in this book has the stamp of the Holy Spirit.

Join the club. It is your call and your destiny.

Amen

LJK

MY BIBLE EXPERIENCE

I installed a 10 foot.satellite dish in my backyard when I lived in Dummer, New Hampshire. I focused my satellite dish on West Star Four, channel 6 and discovered Pastor Murray teaching the Bible.

Approximately ten years ago, I made over six hundred hours of VCR tapes, and I referred to them practically every day. At that time, I was diagnosed with macular degeneration, which stopped me from being able to read. You can now see why I made these tapes.

I have also ordered many CDs and DVDs from the Shepherd's Chapel to help me continue my religious education along with the Shepherd's Chapel's monthly newsletter.

These tapes are a constant source of learning and pleasurable reading for me along with Dr. Murray's Companion Bible: King James Version and with my own life experiences.

THE THOUSAND-YEAR REIGN

The thousand-year reign of Jesus Christ on earth is when we all will be in spiritual bodies. This particular subject was conceived by the Father of the whole earth. After all, he originated the idea of billions of spiritual beings to populate this earth.

The intelligent people of the world have expressed their fear that the world will be destroyed by outer space activities. That notion may be put to rest. Whenever Jesus is present on earth, we are all in heaven in spiritual bodies.

Jesus Christ, our heavenly Father, who made the world to be inhabited, will not let mankind destroy it by nuclear holocaust. He alone can destroy the evil forces. Supernatural events can be only ended by supernatural happenings, and that is our Father, the one who created this world.

What biblically illiterate we mortals be, not to believe the Word of God. I say the forces that will believe the Word of God should reduce their arms output in order for God to do his part, which is to end this war and make the world realize that God has control of our destiny.

Jesus started this war millions of years ago; he is the only one who can stop it. God has all the armor necessary: wind, rain, and weather.

One hundred to one hundred eighty-two pounds of hail stones will decimate some armies. Rain and flood will complete the job.

THE TWO TREES

Two trees were planted in the Garden of Eden: Jesus Planted the tree of life. Satan planted the tree of good and evil.

Jesus planted the taproot of the tree of life deep in the life-producing soil of heaven.

Satan rooted the tree of good and evil in the soil of the abyss, where he will eventually be incarcerated in chains during the millennium for a thousand years. When Satan is released, he will claim those souls who will follow him into the lake of fire.

All human beings are branches of the tree of good and evil. We were all born in sin and come short of the glory of God. That means we all have work to do, which means our homeschooling, if we were brought up in a religious environment, is ahead of the curve.

Many parents joined religious denominations and found out about God in various ways. Over the years, they have settled on those stories that make more sense to them.

In any event, all humans must first repent. Ask *not* what you can do for the Lord, but instead know that you have to repent in order to save your soul.

THE SONG
"HOW GREAT THOU ART"

O Lord my God! When I in awe-some wonder consider all the worlds thy hands have made:

I see the stars
I hear the rolling thunder
Thy power through-out
The universe displayed
When through the woods I wander and hear the brook, and feel the gentle breeze.

(Refrain sung from below)

When I think that God, his son not sparing, sent him to die I can scarcely take it in? On the cross, my burden gladly bearing, he bled and died to take away my sin.

When Christ shall come with shout of acclamation and take me home, what joy shall fill my heart. Then, I shall bow in humble adoration, and there proclaim, my God how great thou art!

(Refrain sung from Below)

REFRAIN

Then sings my soul, my Savior God to thee; how great thou art, how great thou art! Then sings my soul, my Savior God to Thee; how great thou art, How great thou art.

The hymnal from which this song "How Great Thou Art" came was a gift from the following:

The United Methodist Church
Tuttle Road
Cumberland, Maine 04021

I thank you for this gift!

THE HUMAN EXPERIENCE

To become a human being or not is the question. God's "world family" concerning the eight-day man, Adam, and his wife, Eve. Satan, the destroyer and archenemy of Jesus Christ, is known as the tree of good and evil.

The development of the human being is in this order:

1. Skin and bones

2. Sickness

3. Death

These are our destinies.

In other words, there are fruit trees in the garden. The tree of life and the tree of good and evil represent God and Satan and are *not* fruit trees.

The tree of life is Jesus Christ.

The tree of good and evil is Satan.

Spiritual beings can only be eliminated by God. God made the spiritual beings in the first place.

The thought I hope to develop is for the forces of evil who will eventually want to defeat the forces of good that are "God's people" and will give our Savior a reason to begin the battle of Armageddon, which will destroy most of our enemies.

The predicted history of the world has a lot to accomplish before we experience the next phase of history, which will be the battle of Armageddon.

HOW SIN CAME INTO THE
WORLD — THE ORIGINAL SIN

Before I say much more about the original sin, I wish to give the reader more information concerning the six-day man. God created both man and woman at one time and intended them to multiply. All of this took place in the first-world age where few restrictions were placed on embryos.

Satan was very active and was able to convince one-third of God's original embryos to follow him. I figure about seventy billion souls followed Satan. These people went about living their lives for two thousand years.

By the time Adam and Eve committed the original sin, this was an original sin because God had put in place laws to live accordingly.

God told Ha Adam and Eve that if they even touch or eat from the tree of good and evil, they will surely die. Now you know the difference between good and evil or between Satan and God. Which one will you choose?

Now I can talk about the eight-day man "the man, Ha Adam." This is important because the genealogy of Jesus Christ came through this man—Ha Adam. Ha Adam was created from the dust of the earth. Jesus put life in his being and said, "Dust thou are and to dust thou shall return."

The devilish fascination of the human body and the way it plays on the human mind is strictly a mark of Satan's activity. The inability of the human mind to control itself, when looking at the body of the opposite sex, will be the downfall of mankind.

In the beginning, when the Bible talks about the first day with man, it is one thousand years with the Lord. Therefore, the first day is going to last one thousand years, etc. So now, I can mention that at the end of six thousand years, God rested on the seventh day of creation, which was the seventh-thousand years.

Since the beginning of time and the destruction of the first world age, our heavenly Father decided to populate the world with human beings. For that endeavor, he gathered billions of spiritual beings. I will call them embryos in my further discussions.

Our Father's infinite wisdom and knowledge came into question by God when he said in Genesis chapter 6 (in the Bible), that he was sorry he had made man. Only human beings can make human beings. God can make angels and archangels, and he also made the Devil (Satan).

Chapter 28 in the book of Ezekiel describes what Satan will look like when he makes an appearance on earth real soon.

The devil (Satan) will not be a human, although he will pretend to be a human fooling millions of people. God made Satan beautiful. God made him specifically for people to think that he is God.

Satan will be able to do miracles right in front of people. These people will think he is the true God to rapture them away. One of those people could be you if you don't keep up with current Bible knowledge. That knowledge can only be obtained by reading *The Companion Bible: King James Version*, which can be purchased from the following:

http://www.shepherdschapel.com or http://www.amazon.com.

Here is information that may be helpful to you:

Shepherd's Chapel
Pastor Arnold Murray
PO Box 416
Gravette, AR 72736

KANE AND ABEL

God caused Ha Adam to go into a deep sleep. He took a DNA curve from Ha Adam to produce his wife, Eve.

After Eve knew the difference between good and evil, Satan "beguiled" her and "totally seduced" her by emptying his sperms directly into her vagina.

Soon afterward, Ha Adam did the same as Satan did to Eve. Eve then conceived and delivered twin boys. The father of the first boy is Kane, and his descendants are called Kenites. These classes of people are 100 percent for Satan and will fight for him with all of their might. The father of the second boy is Ha Adam, and his son was given the name of Abel. This event with Ha Adam as the prime motivator is the beginning of the descendants of our Savior, Jesus Christ, whose birthday we just celebrated on December 25, 2011

When Kane and Abel became of age, they were to present God with their first fruit.

Kane was a tiller of the soil and gave God a gift that *did not* please Him.

Abel was the keeper of sheep and presented his first fruit as a gift to God, which *was accepted.*

At this time Kane, became jealous of Abel and had him followed into the field and be killed.

Kane married one of the six-day creations who was not one of Ha Adam's children. Eve got pregnant again by her husband, Ha Adam, and called the next son Seth. At this time, the lineage of Ha Adam continues on with Seth.

The genealogy of Kane is in Genesis—chapter four.

The genealogy of Adam is in Genesis—chapter five.

You find in both genealogies the names are very similar to each other. One must *be careful* in distinguishing between these two genealogies.

ORDER OF EVENTS TO COME

1. The battle of Armageddon—the place where the last, decisive battle between the forces of good and evil is to be fought before Judgment Day (Ezekiel 16:16).

2. The tribulation of Satan will last five months, at which time Satan will be the leader of the one-world government.

3. The thousand-year reign is when we will all be spiritual embryos.

4. The tribulation of Satan.

5. The thousand-year reign.

   Note: The only way Satan can be defeated is by God himself.

Mindless individuals are those who think more of lining their pockets or making sure their money stays in their family forever. God said to feed the poor in order to achieve heaven.

The two-party people are misfit individuals who have no compassion for anyone but themselves. They cause confusion and concern about the electoral process. But let us keep them in place, and their presence will aid President Obama to be voted in for a second four-year term in 2012.

The voters of this country would be foolish indeed not to do so.

THE NIMROD COMPLEX

Any individual who in their equation of life does not include the CHRIST who made them is headed for a fall.

I have been given the distinct pleasure of announcing to this present world, present generation that the world will come to an end during President Obama's second term in the White House.

I now feel somewhat like the great EZEKIEL when he met JESUS CHRIST who visited him in in HIS flying saucer by the River Kebar, an accurate description of such an object and I cannot believe so.

Read the first chapter 4 in the Book of Ezekiel and find all about what I am proposing here and now, JUNE 10, 2012, that the Companion Bible is recognized as the true Bible of the Doctrine.

Cowboys for Jesus

THE BATTLE OF ARMAGEDDON
— FROM THE BOOK OF EZEKIEL

I see a period of relative quietness, at which time the democratic nations will reduce their armament to a point that will save them money. This development is our Savior's wish.

At the end of this battle, the world will experience a one-world government headed by Satan. Satan will have a period of five months to play Jesus Christ. God alone will end this war. It will *not* be ours to fight. God will consume them by himself.

The above events I have spoken of will take place during President Obama's second term. President Obama's eloquent way of speaking and his ability to reflect the results in a factual manner will make him a valuable asset to our heavenly Father.

The world's money will be worth nothing, so don't worry. We will become spiritual bodies!

Amen

amen

amen!

Our future is in Jesus

Christ—always was

and

always, always will be.

THE BEGINNING OF SORROWS

Call wolf long enough and eventually no one will believe you.

The gospels of Saint Mark and Saint. Luke have announced the fact that wars and rumors of war will soon come upon the universe, but who will believe such a rumor? The wolf story is too vivid in their thoughts.

Our Father's Holy Spirit has troubled my self-consciousness to be more forthcoming as the prophet Ezekiel to make known to the world that tribulation will soon envelop the whole world. I have been chosen as a "watchman" by the Holy Spirit for the coming of the Antichrist, Satan, and the Man of Sin.

The Tribulation of Satan will last for a period of five months according to the scriptures.

In the eighth and ninth month periods, the Bible talks about the six and seven trumps; it is stated that this period will last a period of five months. This is the time of the Locust Army who will taunt those individuals who have not put the seal of God on their foreheads will be tested.

Satan is coming purposely and peacefully to fool even the most astute and determined Christians.

Many people will be deceived, but thanks to a wonderful and caring Father, the thousand-year reign of Christ on earth is that period of teaching that will result in reclaiming the portion of individuals who at first did not believe.

I am going to lower the boom and tell the world population what is going to take place in the near future. The fig tree was planted in Jerusalem in the year 1948 (Mark 30).

These words are from our Father: "Verily I say unto you that this generation shall not pass till all these things are done." I previously stated that this generation began in 1948 when Israel became a nation. How long does a generation last? Your guess is as good as mine. This is the year 2012; therefore, 1948 to 2012 is sixty-four years. This generation is *already* sixty-four years old.

The chapter thirteen in the gospel of Mark is a treasure of facts concerning the record of God, which each Christian ought to know in order not to be fooled into believing Satan when he claims to be Jesus. He is so good a liar, even God's elect may believe him.

His sinful and degenerating world can no longer be tolerated by our Father. I sense the world coming to a quick end. A famine will soon come upon the world. Not a famine for bread but famine for the word of God. Are you prepared for such an event?

The word of the Lord came again unto me, saying, "Son of man say unto the 'Prince of Tyrus' [Satan] thus saith the Lord God [Satan] because thine heart is lifted up and though hast said, 'I am a God, and I sit in the seat of God in the midst of the seas,' yet though art a man, and not God, though thou set thine heart as the heart of God.

I PLAN TO EQUATE THE "UNIVERSAL SOLVENCY"

Water to the universe.

Salvation and power of Jesus Christ.

Liquid water gives us power to live as humans.

Knowing God gives us power to achieve everlasting life.

Ice and solid water can be considered useless, so to speak, when we compare it to Jesus Christ, who was crucified on a Roman cross and shed his blood for the remission of sin, which allows us to repent, love Jesus, and go straight to heaven.

Water vapor and the Holy Spirit are both present through the world and serve both man and God to accomplish this purpose.

The Hebrew uses the word *huwach* regarding wind when the spirit of God is involved. Now we see that the Holy Spirit has power over the wind to use at his discretion.

I believe, with all my heart and soul, that Yashua Messiah Jesus Christ, the son of Living God, wants to end this war as soon as possible. This war cannot be won by human beings. God alone has to end it.

At the very beginning of the millennium, the thousand-year reign of Jesus Christ will begin on this earth.

A sentence was made in the Bible: "That every Knee shall bow and every Heart shall confess that Jesus Christ is LORD."

Since this is a future event, some other event must take place. The next thing scheduled to happen is the tribulation of Satan. Satan will claim to be Jesus Christ and rule this earth for a period of five months. During this time, the world will function as a one-world government with Satan as the head.

I would keep away from all ministers who teach only "born again" and speaking in tongues as good teaching techniques that will get one into heaven. They teach the rapture theory and real theory, but they are false. This was surfaced back in 1830 by a woman who was mentally sick. The ministers who were present thought they had reached the mother lode and presented it as real.

I say leave the homosexuals alone as they have their own cross to bear but have no idea how they became that way. The various denominations have always condemned them. I think homosexuals and pedophiles in the church system believe the reason is to keep the general public from finding out about their own pedophilia and homosexuality.

Those priests molested many innocent young boys, which was kept a secret. One can see we are all guilty of everything we accuse others of doing. *No one is perfect.* Let God be God. Let him chart our future.

God has noted our future in "his Word" and detailed every event in the wonderful book of Ezekiel.

This present war was started by God himself. In the first world age, millions of years ago, when we were all in embryo stage of spiritual life, God decided to populate that world age with individuals he had created. They turned out to be sinners of every sort, so God destroyed the first world age by a terrible shaking to it, and it sank out of sight in the waters that surrounded it.

Many biblically illiterate people confuse this event with Noah's flood. The fourth chapter in the book of Jeremiah describes the destruction of the first world age.

In the great book of Ezekiel, around about chapter 37, it talks about the dry bones, which is a total restoration of both houses of Israel. Believe it or not, the house of Israel, which is really the people who were promised that Abraham's descendants, would reap the rewards. This is coming true and they will be first in the inner sanctuary of Jesus Christ during the millennium. At that particular time, every knee shall bow, every heart shall confess that Jesus is the Son of God, and that is what God wants to prove above all. Right now, the house of Israel is divided up into two houses and will be joined together as God's promise in his word, and they will be seated with Jesus Christ to rule this world.

Those who have already died are in heaven without any *rapture theory* whatsoever and the traditions of men who confuse the Bible to the extent that nobody can understand it, which will complicate matters a great deal.

After the tribulation of Satan has been taught for a thousand years, by the time that teaching is done, in my opinion, not only millions but billions of people will come to know God better. Billions of people will be saved at the end of the thousand-year reign.

We will all be in spiritual bodies. We will need a lot of friends that we have known who will be become teachers during the thousand-year reign. I am so eager for this to come about.

There are various forms of education; we have to look forward to the time Jesus is on earth during the thousand-year reign.

The book of Ezekiel from chapter 38 through chapter 44 will tell you who will win the war and how the war is won. The people nowadays are going to go broke because of spending money trying to end the war. Blood and guts cannot win this war.

I will try to be more specific as to where these places are found in the Bible. You will be able to look them up if you're so inclined to read them. If you're not inclined to read these things, you're going to listen to a bunch of traditions of men who know absolutely nothing concerning the Bible, and it's going to confuse everybody.

This is an open letter to all that I hope will read this book and consider early because it's going to happen regardless of what they think.

Now if any thinking person is present, it is soon apparent that God has set up a situation that will eventually make the world realize that Christ Jesus will triumph when this world ceases to exist.

The two-party organization a desperate attempt by desperate people to line their own pockets. This is a sad, sad, sad situation.

Our Father is not slow in making up his mind to counter conditions in the world. As they exist, there is an appointed scheduled time for anything he deems necessary to accomplish. Take the situation when he told the four angels to hold the four winds until the one hundred thousand members repented of their sins were sealed by God before it became too late for such an action. Now I say this: God can control the weather anytime he needs to accomplish his will.

Our Father is sick of this world. The gibberish talk that leads to nowhere solves no problems. God has his angels flying UFOs to report conditions in the world, and I tell you now, it will not be long before he pulls the plug on us.

WHAT IS THE NORMAL PERSON TO DO?

Fill your sinful body with drugs, or play it straight and repent for your sins and make an attempt to save your soul. Do it the smart way. You may not have many more chances. We are all sinners the very day we were born, and some even before we were born.

Ask not what you can do for the Lord, but instead know that you have to repent to save your soul, for we are all sinners.

AN OPEN LETTER TO THE PRESIDENT OF THE UNITED STATES, PRESIDENT BARACK OBAMA

I believe God has given you a new mandate—to win this war as fast as possible.

Due to your eloquent way of speaking, you are requested to convenience all the world leaders that blood, guts, and all the world ammunition cannot end this war!

Jesus started this war millions of years ago; he is the only one who can stop it. He has all the armor necessary: wind, rain, and weather.

One hundred to one hundred eighty-two pounds of hailstones will decimate some armies. Rain and flood will complete the job.

I plan to recommend Dr. Arnold Murray to you, President Obama, as your spiritual advisor. I believe that if you choose Dr. Arnold Murray as your spiritual advisor, you will always be ahead of the curve when dealing with end-time events.

I believe also that you would like to have a six-foot five inch three-hundred-pound US marine wearing size 13 shoes as your spiritual adviser!

AN OPEN LETTER TO DR. ARNOLD MURRAY

Pastor, Shepherd's Chapel in Gravette, Arkansas

The only difference between your theologies and mine is that I eat a

Jimmy Dean—sausage, egg, and cheese
biscuit—practically every day.

I plan to live until Christ comes, and I hope to see you there
also. I appreciate all I have learned from you, and it has
enlightened me far more than I ever thought. Thank you!

Isn't *God* terrific. I love him so much.

APPENDIX

FIG TREE REFERENCES

MARK 13

28: "Now learn a parable of the fig tree; When her branches are still tender and bring forth leaves, ye know that summer is near." (Seven seals is harvesttime.)

29: "So in like manner, when ye shall see these things come to past [fig tree planted in 1984] know that it is nigh, even at the doors."

30: "Verily I say unto you, that this generation shall not pass, till all these things be done." (This earth age—all seven seals.)

31: "Heaven and earth shall pass away, but my words shall not pass away." (This earth age.)

32: "But of that day, and that hour knoweth no man. No not the angels which are in heaven; Neither the SON. Only the FATHER will know."

33: "Take ye heed, watch and pray."

JEREMIAH 24

1: "Two baskets of Figs were set before the temple of the LORD."

2: "One basket had very good figs, and the other basket had very naughty figs-which could not be eaten. They were so bad [Kenites]."

5: "Thus sayeth the LORD the GOD of ISRAEL, like these good figs, so will I acknowledge them that are carried away captive of JUDAH whom I have set out of this place into the hands of the CHANDEANS for their good and I will bring them into this land."

6: "For I will set MY eyes upon them for good, and I will bring them again to this land, and I will PLANT them, and not pluck them up."

7: "And I will give them a heart to know ME."

What do *seals*, *plagues*, and *trumps* have to do with the end time?

Revelation 6 gives the appearance of Satan (the *Antichrist*): "He had a bow in his hand and a crown was given to him and he went forth to conquer."

The mark of Satan is 666, which equals the six seals, six trumps, and six vials.

THE SEVEN SPIRITS OF GOD

Revelation 5:12: "Worthy is the Lamb who was slain to receive power and riches and wisdom and strength and honor and glory and blessings."

Isaiah 45:18: "GOD Himself who formed the earth and made it, and established it. He created it not in vain. HE formed it to be inhabited I am the LORD and there is none else."

OTHER REFERENCES

The book of Jeremiah, chapter 4, starting with verse 24, tells about the destruction of the first world age.

If one is really interested in the intricate knowledge of the Bible, one must have the companion version of the Bible.

ISAIAH 14

12: "How art though fallen from Heaven O Lucifer—Son of the morning. How are thou cut down to the ground, which didst weaken the nations?"

13: "For you have said in thine heart, 'I will ascend into Heaven; I will exalt my throne above the throne of God.' I will sit also upon the mount of the congregations, in the sides of the North [Satan]."

14: "I will ascent above the heights of the clouds, I will be like the Most High [Satan]."

15: "Yet thou shalt be brought down to Hell, to the sides of the pit [Satan]."

16: "They that see thee in the pit shall narrowly look upon thee, and consider thee, saying, 'Is this the man who made the earth to tremble, that did shake Kingdoms [Satan].'"

EZEKIEL

The Battle of Armageddon

39:1: Therefore, son of man, prophesy against Gog, and say, "thus saith the LORD GOD, Behold I am against thee, O Gog, the Chief Prince Meshach and Tubal.

39:2: "And I will turn thee back, and leave but the sixth part of three, and I will cause thee to come up from the North Parts and will bring the upon the Mountains of Israel."

39:3: "And I will smite thy bow out of thy left hand, and I will cause thine arrows to fall out of the right hand."

39:4: "Thou shall fall upon the Mountains of Israel, and all thy bands, and the people that are with thee. I will give these into the ravenous birds of every sort and to the breasts on the fields to be devoured."

39:5: "Thou shalt upon the open fields: for I have spoken it, saith the Lord God."

BEGUILE

Genesis 3:30 "Eve said, "That Satan beguiled me.""

2 Corinthians 11:3: "But I am afraid that just as Eve was deceived by the serpent's cunning, your minds may somehow be led astray from your sincere and pure devotion to Christ."

Verse 1818 in the Greek Dictionary means to seduce wholly, beguile, and deceive

The word touch – Hebrew 3:3 page 5060 – means to sleep with a woman.

(From Strong's Concordance of the Bible, Hebrew Section 5060)

Revelations 14:3: "And they sang the Song of Moses, the servant of the Lord and the Song of the Lamb."

Deuteronomy 21:22: "Moses therefore wrote this song the same day and taught it to the Children of Israel."

Deuteronomy 32:1: "[Moses] Give ear, O ye heavens and I will speak, and hear O earth, the words of my mouth."

Deuteronomy 32:2: "My doctrine shall drop as the rain, my speech shall distill as the dew, as the small rain upon the tender herb. And as showers fall on the grass."

Deuteronomy 32:3: "Because I will publish the Name of the Lord; Ascribe ye greatness unto our God."

Deuteronomy 32:4: "He is the Rock, HIS work is perfect: For all HIS ways is Judgment. A GOD of truth and Inequity. Just and right is HE."

Deuteronomy 32:5: "They have corrupted themselves, their spot is not the spot of his children; they are a perverse and crooked generation."

Deuteronomy 32:6: "Do ye thus requite the LORD? O foolish people and unwise. Is not he they FATHER that had bought thee? Hath I not made thee and established thee?"

Deuteronomy 32:7: "Remember the days of old? Consider the years of many generations. Ask they father and he will show thee, Thy Elders, and they will tell Thee."

Deuteronomy 32:8: "When the MOST HIGH divides to the nations their inheritance. When HE separated the sons of, he set the bounds of the people, according to the number of the Children of Israel."

Deuteronomy 32:9: "For the LORD is HIS people; Jacob is the lot of HIS inheritance."

Deuteronomy 32:10: "HE found him in a desert land; that is the waste howling wilderness. HE led Him about, He instructed Him, and HE kept Him as the Apple of HIS eye."

Deuteronomy 32:11: "As an eagle stirred up her nest, fluttered over her young, spreadeth her wings, taketh them, and beareth them on their wings."

Deuteronomy 32:12: "So the Lord alone did lead him and there was no strange GOD with him."

Deuteronomy 32:13: "HE made him ride on the high places of the earth, that he might eat the increase of the fields and HE made him to suck honey out of the rock and oil out of the flinty rock."

Deuteronomy 32:14: "Butter of kine and milk of sheep with fat of lambs, fruitful, and rams of the Breed of Bashan and Goats, with the fat of Kidneys of Wheat, and thou didst drink the pure blood of the grape, The True CHRIST!"

Deuteronomy 32:15: "But Jeshurun waxed fat and kicked. Thou art waxen fat, thou art grown thick, and thou art covered with fatness. Then HE forsook GOD which made him, and lightly esteemed the ROCK of his salvation."

Deuteronomy 32:16: "They provoked HIM to jealous with strange gods."

BIOGRAPHY OF LOUIS J. KEROACK

I was born in Berlin, New Hampshire, on April 6, 1920. My parents migrated down from Canada to become US Citizens. They operated a grocery store at 136 Bridge Street in Berlin, New Hampshire.

My father, Earnest Keroack, and mother, Mederise Quintal Keroack, had three children, and I am the second of the three children. My father died at the age of ninety-one and dispatched directly into the arms of Jesus. My sister, Claire, recently died at age ninety-four and was an avid listener of the Boston Red Sox She was a teller in the Berlin Bank of New Hampshire.

My brother, Robert, became a cook during the Second World War. He operated a hotel in Newport, Vermont, and later died because of his army-service experiences.

My grandfather Quintal built a large three-story building with a large grocery store in the bottom of this building on the corner of Goble Street. His children occupied the first two levels and worked in the grocery store. My grandfather died of pleurisy at an early age.

His wife, my grandmother, died at the age of 102 after raising thirteen children and was dispatched into the arms of Jesus Christ.

The parochial school I attended was called the Guardian Angel School and was run by nuns. We learned French in the morning and English in the afternoon. While at school, I shimmed up a twenty five- or thirty-foot wooden flag pole and retrieved an American flag that was hooked on a spike on the top of the pole. I later entered Berlin High School in 1935. While in high school at age seventeen, I took advantage of a government program and spent a month becoming a Soldier at Fort Williams off the shore of Portland, Maine. This program became quite an experience for me; this was my first train ride and my first look at the Atlantic Ocean and the Casco Bay Islands.

Further on in my school life, I applied for a government flying program that would become successful. I had to fly seventy-five hours in a powered aircraft, and upon completion, I received my private pilot's license while I was in my senior year in high school.

In 1939, I was taking a mechanical arts program. I had an opportunity to play hockey, which I enjoyed very much. During this period of life, I fell deeply in love with a beautiful young lady by the name of Doris Danis. She was a junior in high school. In my own mind, I planned to ask her to marry me. The Lord had other plans for my life, which I knew nothing about. Soon afterward, I fell *completely out of love.*

This is a new year—January 2012. I will be ninety-two years old in April, although a babe in Christ Jesus. I must get the lead out and finish this book.

I started dating a beautiful lady by the name of Isabelle Ann Derby, who was one and one and a half years older than I. I was drafted while working in the machine shop in 1942 and shipped to Fort Devens, Massachusetts for assignment. My girlfriend joined the Woman's Army Auxiliary Corporation (WAAC) and, upon completing her service, was assigned at the Pentagon in Washington DC as a stenographer working for visiting generals.

Fort Myer, Virginia

Meanwhile, I had become a glider pilot and received my flight training in Hamilton, Texas. I was shipped to Seattle, Washington, for B-29 training; I received a thirty-day delay in route and contacted my girlfriend at her base near the Pentagon, and we were married there.

When the war ended, my wife and I applied for college under the GI Bill. We enrolled at the University of New Hampshire in 1946 and graduated in 1950. I got a BS degree in mechanical engineering and my wife got a BS degree in geology.

While teaching at Wentworth Institute in Boston, Massachusetts, I attended a teachers' college and received my master's degree in school administration. My wife went on to receive her master's degree in library science. By this time, we had acquired the proper credentials and began teaching at the Vocational Technical Community College in Berlin, New Hampshire, now known as White Mountain Community College.

During our summer vacations, my wife and I began in 1970 to travel the world from Canada, Norway, Sweden, Japan, and all points in between. I joined the Full Gospel Business Men Fellowship International. I then started a chapter in the Berlin and Gorham New, Hampshire areas of the Full Gospel Business Men's Fellowship. We had monthly meetings at the Town and Country Motor Inn in Shelburne, New Hampshire.

OUR HOST: TOWN & COUNTRY MOTOR INN

After Ann and I had been married for sixty years, I thanked God for his Word: "I shall never leave thee nor forsake thee."

My wife departed for heaven in April 2004 after suffering from Lou Gehrig's disease or amyotrophic lateral sclerosis (ALS).

Our Father, the living God, must have determined long ago that I would be under dire circumstances if I did not find the correct life companion. God gave me a sixty-four-year-old angel by the name of Sandy.

Unbeknownst to me, the Lord placed "my wife-to-be," Sandra (Sandy) Stanley—age fifty-nine who grew up in Falmouth, Maine, and purchased a condominium adjacent to mine at approximately the same time Ann and I did. Sandy and Ann had a *very special* friendship throughout Ann's life here in Falmouth Colonial Village, Falmouth, Maine. They got to know each other because of Ann's love of cats, and Sandy had a Maine Coon tiger cat, which Ann loved to the very end!

Sandy was one of eight children (six boys and two girls.) Growing up in Falmouth, Maine, Sandy enjoyed swimming in the nearby ocean beach, sailboating (sailboats made by her Dad for the children), snowshoeing, skiing, skating with wood fires made by her Dad on the island in the middle of the Pond, and the many friendships she made in school and out.

We got married by a wonderful minister, Rev. C. Richard Sheesley, on August 12, 2006, in Portland, Maine, in a beautiful setting on the Eastern Promenade in a gazebo overlooking Casco Bay, with relatives and friends joining us in this special occasion.

Sandy started her accounting business in June 1980 and has enjoyed thirty-two years assisting others with their accounting needs along with traveling, scuba diving, and flying. Sandy is a very thoughtful person and makes me feel safe and enjoy our life together!

With all my heart, I believe that God will never leave us nor forsake us.

Amen!

THE TRIBES OF ISRAEL

1. Reuben
2. Simeon
3. Levi
4. Judah
5. Dan
6. Naphtali
7. Gad
8. Asher
9. Issachar
10. Zebulun
11. Joseph
12. Benjamin

PUBLISHER INFORMATION REQUEST

The wisdom of man says, "I guess this event may happen in the future." The wisdom of God says, "This event will happen in its appropriate time."

God made Ha Adam, and all generations to follow would be called God's people and be blessed by him.

MSNBC's *The Ed Show* and *The Rachel Maddow Show*, CNN's *GPS* show, and The NECN shows—these are places I would like to attend with my book.

In the industrial world, your worth is determined by the amount of your paycheck.

In religion, your worth is determined by your faith, and your faith is rewarded by your work.

Salvation is available to whosoever will.

I would like to have the web site:
http://www.TwoTreesofDestinyChristVersesSatan.com.

ACKNOWLEDGMENTS

To Michele, VA, Togus, Maine, for assisting me in equipment to be able to accomplish the following: learn to type at ninety-one years young to write this book (*wow*), be able to read with enhanced vision equipment, *live a life safely and as full as possible with macular degeneration*. Thank you for having such patience and knowledge in working with me.

To Sandy Keroack, my wife, for helping me in putting this book together, her patience and determination to keep me working to finish this book, and her computer knowledge and abilities.

Xlibris Publishing: To Rey Soriano, we felt like you were helping us every step of the way. Your patience, understanding, and expertise are above and beyond anything I expected. To James Calonia (manuscript service representative) and Kris Alberto (submissions representative), thank you for your patience, understanding, and help along my journey with this book. Xlibris has a wonderful, courteous staff and we thank each of you for your expertise!

Thank you to family and friends who listened as I went through this journey and helped to keep me focused with their encouragement.

CPSIA information can be obtained at www.ICGtesting.com
Printed in the USA
BVOW021931120912

300185BV00001B/4/P